SUPERIFIC SCIENCE

CHEMISTRY CONCEPTS

by
Lorraine Conway

Illustrated by Linda Akins

Cover by Kathryn Hyndman

Copyright © Good Apple, Inc., 1983

ISBN No. 0-86653-100-9

Good Apple, Inc.
299 Jefferson Road
P.O. Box 480
Parsippany, NJ 07054-0480

TABLE OF CONTENTS

INTRODUCTION

We live in a chemical world. The food we eat, the clothes we wear, the homes we live in, the automobiles we drive, and the medicine we use to fight disease and expand our lives are in many ways linked to chemistry. *Chemistry Concepts* was written to provide a beginning to the understanding of the enormous and ever-growing field of chemistry, a most exciting science.

Acknowledgement:

Special appreciation to Garth Forster, chemistry teacher at Wheeler High School, Marietta, Georgia, for reading the manuscript and offering his suggestions.

MATTER

Look around you and make a list of ten different things in the room. All of the things on your list are matter. Your pencil and pens, the books and furniture in the room, the air you breathe, the food you eat and the liquids you drink, as well as the animals, plants and people around you, are examples of matter. Matter is anything that has weight and takes up space. The three forms of matter are solids, liquids and gases. Rocks, metals, glass, and trees are a few examples of solid matter. Water, milk, and oil are liquid matter; the air you breathe and the gases you exhale are matter in gaseous form.

Some types of matter can be found in all three forms. Water is a good example of this. Under normal conditions water is a liquid; when temperatures drop below 0° C or 32° F, water turns into a solid, ice. When water is heated to temperatures above 100° C or 212° F, it will begin to boil and produce steam. Steam is water in the form of a gas. Water vapor in the air is also a gas which we call humidity.

Carbon dioxide is a gas in its normal state. In very low temperatures it changes into the solid form that we call dry ice. It has been given this name because it skips the wet stage and does not melt as ordinary ice does; instead it goes directly from a solid into the air as a gas.

Iron is usually a solid; under very high temperature it becomes liquid or molten as do many other metals. Mercury, the silver substance found in some thermometers, is a liquid in its natural state.

MATTER

Indicate whether the following examples are solid, liquid or gaseous states of matter.

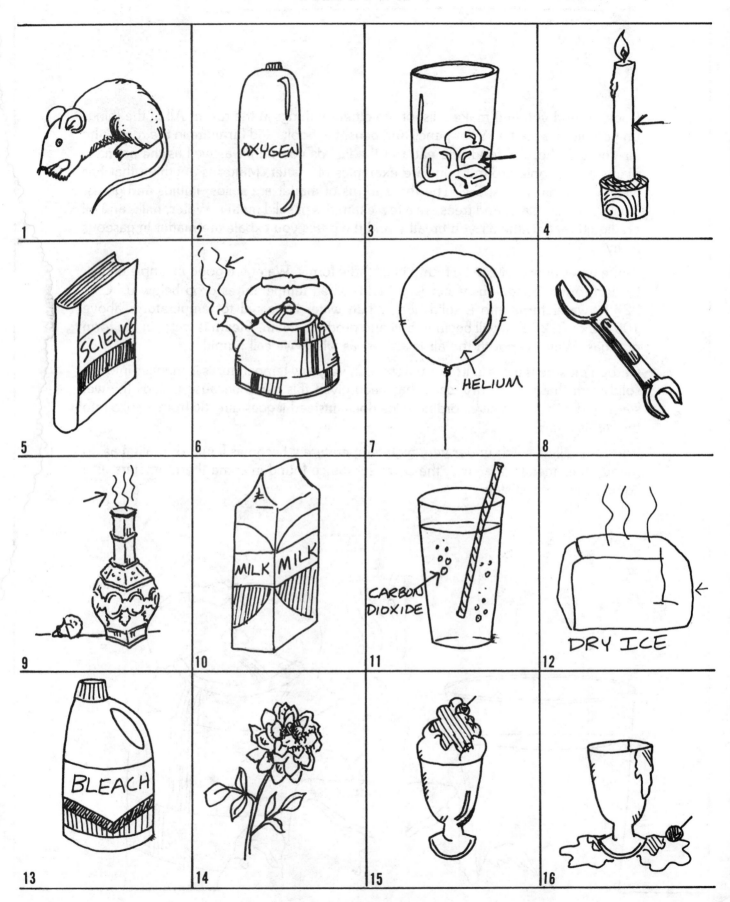

STATES OF MATTER

How many examples of each of the three states of matter can you find in the picture?

3

MOLECULES AND MATTER

All matter is made of molecules. If you keep breaking a substance down into smaller and smaller pieces, the smallest piece into which you can break it into and still have a portion of that substance is a molecule. The molecules of solids, liquids and gases differ from each other. In solids the molecules are very close together and they move very slowly. In liquids the molecules pick up speed and are farther apart. In gases the molecules move very swiftly and have large spaces between them.

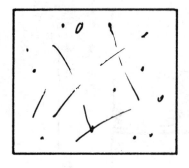 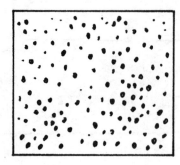 

Can you identify the solid, liquid and the gas in the above blocks of matter? Complete the following statements:

1. All matter is made of _____ .

2. The smallest part into which you can break matter and still have some substance is a _____ .

3. Molecules are always _____ .

4. The molecules of solids, liquids and gases _____ from each other.

MOLECULES ARE ALWAYS MOVING

A good way to illustrate the fact that molecules are always moving is to do the following activity:

Materials: Beaker or jar, red food coloring, water, eyedropper

Procedure: Into a glass of water put a few drops of red food coloring. Allow this mixture to stand undisturbed. After awhile the jar will be evenly colored as the molecules of water and the molecules of food coloring move throughout the solution.

Question: What properties of molecules enabled the food coloring to tint the water?

MOLECULES FROM ATOMS

To give students a clearer understanding of how molecules are made from atoms, do the following activity:

Materials: Quarter-sized circles of construction paper; for each student or pair of students, you will need:

1 carbon	(1 black circle)
3 hydrogen	(3 white circles)
7 oxygen	(7 red circles)
1 chlorine	(1 green circle)
1 nitrogen	(1 orange circle)
1 sulphur	(1 yellow circle)

Toothpicks for bonds
Use each circle to represent one atom.

Procedure: Using the above key and given the following formulas, the students will build the following molecules:

CO_2	carbon dioxide
H_2O	water
NO_2	nitrogen dioxide
SO_2	sulfur dioxide
HCl	hydrochloric acid

Each formula indicates one molecule. If a scientist wants to indicate two molecules of a substance, he would put a 2 before the molecular formula as $2CO_2$, meaning two molecules of carbon dioxide.

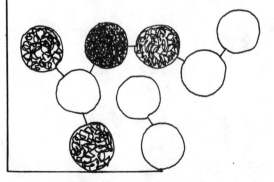

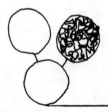

MOLECULES FROM ATOMS

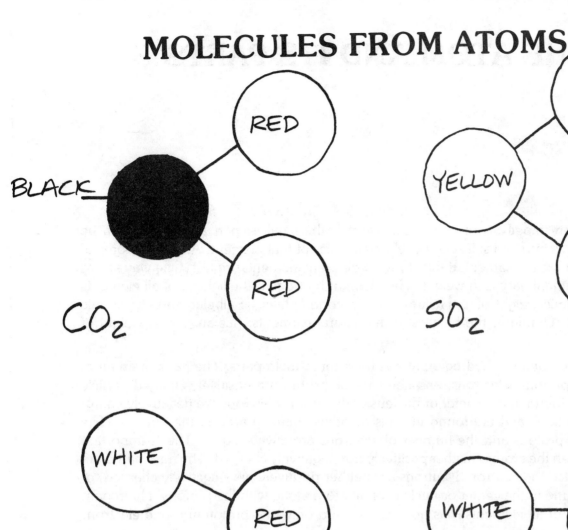

CO₂

SO₂

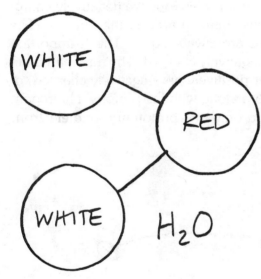

H₂O

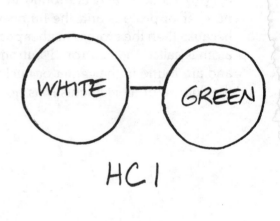

HCl

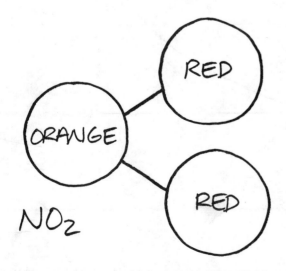

NO₂

QUESTIONS:

1. A molecule of carbon dioxide is made of one atom of _____ and two of _____.
2. A molecule of water is made from two atoms of _____ and one of _____.
3. A molecule of nitrogen dioxide is made of one atom of _____ and two of _____.
4. A molecule of sulfur dioxide is made of one atom of _____ and two of _____.
5. A molecule of hydrochloric acid is made of one atom of _____ and one of _____.

7

THE ATOM AND ITS PARTS

Elements are made up of atoms. An atom is the smallest part an element can be broken down into and still keep the characteristics of that element. All of the atoms of an element are the same; but the atoms of different elements are not. One way atoms of each element vary is in weight. The element hydrogen, the lightest of all elements has an atomic weight of 1. Helium is the second lightest of all elements. Its atomic weight is 4. Uranium, the heaviest of all natural elements, has an atomic weight of 238.

With the exception of hydrogen, atoms have three main parts. The parts of an atom are called protons, electrons, and neutrons. A proton is a positively charged particle (+) and is found in the center or nucleus of the atom. Electrons are negatively charged (−) particles and are found in rings or orbits spinning around the nucleus. The number of protons and the number of electrons are always equal. This is important because then the atom is neither positively nor negatively charged. The third part of an atom is called the neutron. Neutrons are neither positively nor negatively charged (o) and are found in the center or nucleus of an atom along with the protons. Hydrogen, the lightest of all elements, has no neutrons and only one proton and one electron.

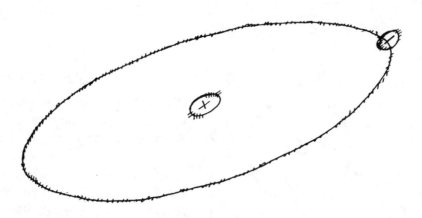

Protons and neutrons are the heavy parts of an atom and their combined weights are called the atomic weight of an element. Electrons are so very light that we say they do not have weight.

Use the table below as a self-check to see if you understand about protons, neutrons and electrons.

ATOMIC PART	WEIGHT		CHARGE			WHERE FOUND	
	Yes	No	Positive	Negative	Neutral	Inside Nucleus	Outside Nucleus
PROTON							
NEUTRON							
ELECTRON							

Study the drawings below. Answer the questions at the bottom of the page.

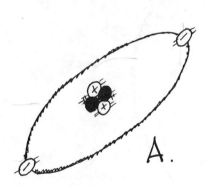

A.

B.

Questions:
1. How many protons are there in the A atom? _____ the B atom? _____
2. How many neutrons are there in the B atom? _____ the A atom? _____
3. How many electrons are there in the A atom? _____ the B atom? _____
4. What is the atomic weight of atom B? _____ of atom A? _____
5. What is element A? _____
6. What is element B? _____

BUILDING ATOMS

To familiarize students with such terms as atom, electron, proton, neutron, shell, atomic weight, and atomic number, do the following activity.

Materials: Squares of corrugated paper, the size depending upon the size of the atoms the teacher wishes the students to build. Thumbtacks and pen or pencils are also needed. The thumbtacks must be in three different colors: one color represents electrons, one color protons, and another color neutrons.

Procedure: On the squares of corrugated paper the students make their atoms by inserting thumbtacks of one color into the center for the locations of protons. If the atom contains neutrons, these are added to the center by using tacks of a different color. Have students draw rings around the nucleus for the shells of the electrons, and use a third color of tacks for the electrons. The first shell or path of electrons around the nucleus is called the K shell, and it can only hold up to two electrons. The second shell, called the L shell, holds up to eight electrons. There can be as many as eighteen electrons in the third shell which is called the M shell, while the maximum number in the fourth or N shell is thirty-two.

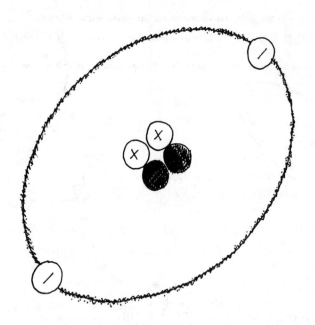

A HELIUM ATOM

BUILDING ATOMS

Use the information in the table below to build model atoms of those elements represented.

ELEMENT	NUMBER OF PROTONS	NUMBER OF NEUTRONS	NUMBER OF ELECTRONS
Hydrogen	1	0	1
Helium	2	2	2
Aluminum	13	14	13
Oxygen	8	8	8
Beryllium	4	5	4

Remember: Protons have a positive (+) charge.
Electrons have a negative (−) charge.
Neutrons have no charge ($\pm$) or (o)

Protons and neutrons have weight; therefore, the atomic weight of an atom is the sum of the protons and neutrons. The atomic number of an atom is the number of protons in its nucleus.

Questions: 1. What is the atomic number of the atom you have made?
2. What is its atomic weight?
3. How can you tell the atomic weight?
4. Why is the number of protons and the number of electrons of an atom equal?

CHEMISTRY EQUIPMENT

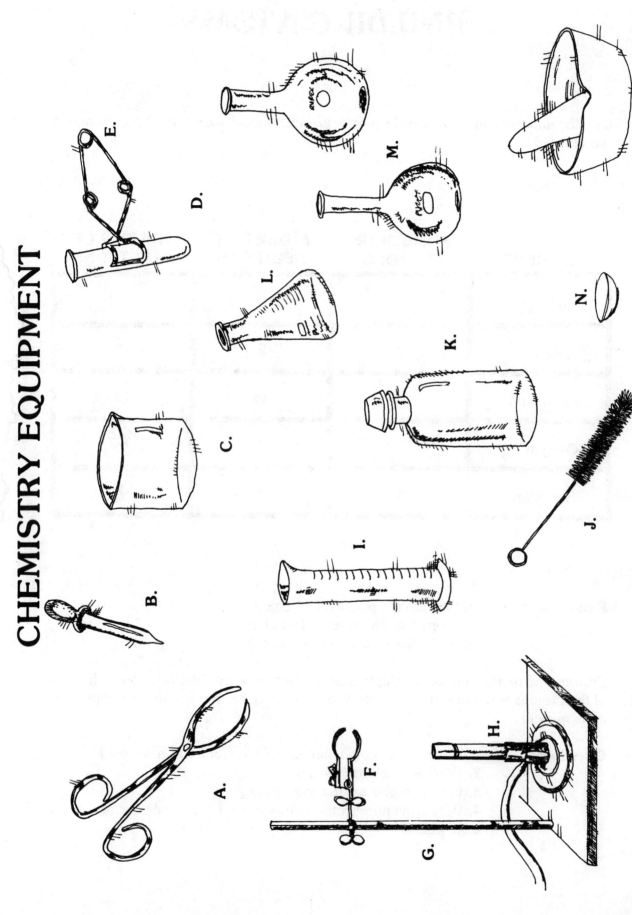

The following pieces of equipment could be found on the chemist's lab table: mortar and pestle, watch glass, test tube, Bunsen burner, reagent bottle, Erlenmeyer flask, test tube holder, Florence flasks, beaker, pipette (eyedropper), test tube brush, ring stand, graduated cylinder, tongs, clamp. Can you identify each?

USING FILTER PAPER

In chemistry you will use filter paper often. To use it correctly, it must be folded carefully. The proper way to fold filter paper is shown below. Practice filtering with a piece of filter paper and a mixture of sand and water.

A. Start with a piece of filter paper.

B. Fold the circle of paper exactly in half.

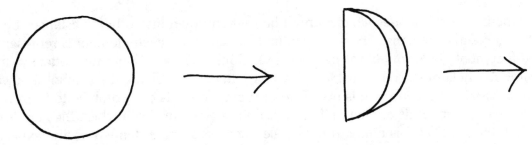

C. Fold it in half a second time.

D. Make a cone of three sides and one side. Fit it snugly into a funnel.

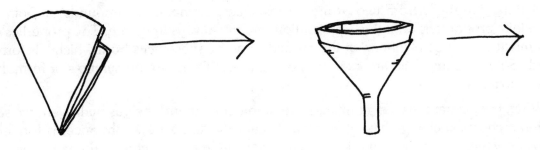

E. Practice filtering a mixture of sand and water.

F. A useful tip to keep the liquid from running down the side of the container and spilling is to use a clean stirring rod to direct the liquid as shown.

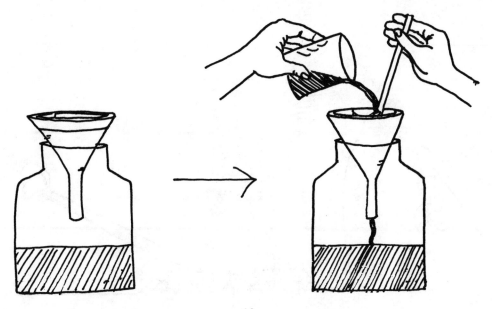

ELEMENTS, COMPOUNDS, AND MIXTURES

Elements are substances which cannot be broken down into other substances by ordinary chemical means. There are about 100 elements; each element is represented by a symbol. The symbol for oxygen is O. Some elements have two letters in their symbols; helium's symbol is He. The first letter in an element's symbol is always capitalized, the second one is not. Two or more elements can combine to form compounds. Compounds are very different from the elements from which they are formed. Table salt (NaCl) is made from two elements: sodium, a dangerous and explosive element, and chlorine, a poisonous gas. The elements which compose compounds exist in definite proportions and are always the same; for this reason we are able to write formulas for compounds such as NaCl for salt and H_2O for water.

Mixtures are made from two or more substances, elements, compounds, or both in definite proportions, and these proportions are not always the same. The properties of a mixture are a combination of the properties of the substances from which it is formed. Soil, cake and milk are examples of mixtures. There are no symbols or formulas for mixtures.

When the element oxygen combines with another element, the gas hydrogen, we say that a chemical change has taken place because water, a new substance, is formed. When water is broken down into oxygen and hydrogen, a chemical change occurs also because oxygen and hydrogen are formed. A change in a substance which does not alter the chemical makeup of the substance is called a physical change. Breaking a bottle is an example of a physical change; the bottle has certainly changed, but no new chemical substances are formed.

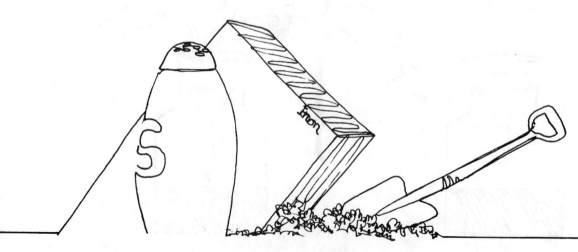

14

ROTATION LAB ON ELEMENTS, COMPOUNDS, AND MIXTURES

In this lab students will learn the difference between an element, compound, and a mixture.

Materials: Examples of some common elements such as copper, iron, lead, mercury (a mercury thermometer can be used with an arrow pointing to the mercury), aluminum, sulfur, iodine crystals, magnesium, etc. Examples of compounds may include water, salt, sugar, peroxide, rust, and other available compounds. Good examples of mixture are soil, air, steel, and pepper. Whistle or clicker to signal change.

Procedure: In a rotation each student is assigned a numbered station, and each student has an answer sheet on which to record his findings. The students will change stations at intervals depending upon the length of time needed to record their answers. All students change stations at the same time at a given signal from the teacher. The signal may be a word, a whistle, or a click. At the signal the student at station one goes to station two, two goes to three, etc., each student proceeding to the next highest number with the exception of the student at the highest numbered station, who proceeds to station one.

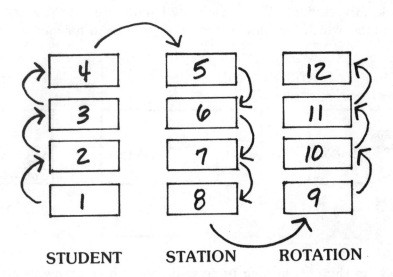

STUDENT   STATION   ROTATION

The teacher keeps track of the time. One to two minutes per station is usually sufficient for the rotation lab on elements, compounds, and mixtures.

At each station (desk) have an example of either an element, compound or mixture. Supply only the name of the sample if it is a mixture; its name and symbol if it is an element; and its name and formula if it is a compound.

EXAMPLES:

NAME: ⊛ SYMBOL:	NAME: ╱ NO SYMBOL
COPPER CU	AIR OR FORMULA

The student will copy the given information on the answer sheet and will proceed to answer the remainder of the information on his own.

(Note: Each student begins at his station number on his answer sheet. Only number one begins at number one of the answer sheet, number two at number two, etc.)

The students should soon begin to understand that elements are made of one substance, that compounds have two or more, and that mixtures are composed of several substances in indefinite proportions, and no symbol or formula can be written for them. If elements, compounds, and mixtures are provided in the solid, liquid, and gaseous states, the student will be enlightened in this area, also. When possible, try to provide elements which combine to form compounds in a sequence. For example:

NAME: ☁ SYMBOL:	NAME ☁ SYMBOL:	NAME: ● FORMULA
IRON Fe	SULFER S	IRON SULFIDE FeS

This will aid the students in their understanding of how elements combine to form compounds, which are entirely different substances.

ROTATION LAB ON ELEMENTS, COMPOUNDS, AND MIXTURES

Name of Substance	Symbol or Formula	Color	Check One			Check One		
			Solid	Liquid	Gas	Element	Compound	Mixture
1.								
2.								
3.								
4.								
5.								
6.								
7.								
8.								
9.								
10.								
11.								
12.								
13.								
14.								
15.								
16.								
17.								
18.								
19.								
20.								
21.								
22.								
23.								
24.								
25.								
26.								
27.								

A PHYSICAL AND CHEMICAL CHANGE

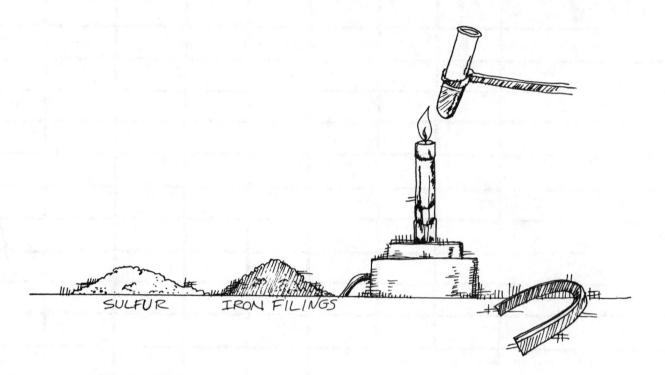

SULFUR   IRON FILINGS

Materials: Powdered sulfur, iron filings, magnet, test tube, towel or cloth, Bunsen burner, test tube holder, matches, hammer or mallet.

Procedure: Mix equal amounts of powdered sulfur and iron filings, about two tablespoons of each. Pass a magnet over this mixture. Describe what happens.

Is this a physical or chemical change? How do you know? Scrape the iron filings from the magnet and again mix the iron with sulfur. Pour some of this mixture into a test tube. Using a test tube holder, carefully heat this mixture over a Bunsen burner until contents begin to glow. Allow test tube to cool. Wrap the test tube in a towel or rag and carefully tap with a hammer. Remove the contents of the test tube. Pass a magnet over the iron and sulfur.

Describe what happens now.

Is this a physical or chemical change? How do you know?

PHYSICAL OR CHEMICAL CHANGE?

Tell whether each of the following pictures represents a physical or chemical change by circling the appropriate letter.

Crushing a rock	**Rusting of iron**	**Seltzer tablet in water**
P or C	P or C	P or C
Slicing bread	**Digestion of food**	**Baking bread**
P or C	P or C	P or C
Tearing a piece of paper	**Burning a candle**	**Steam from boiling water**
P or C	P or C	P or C

CHEMICAL SYMBOLS

Each element has its own symbol. Symbols are a chemist's shorthand. In writing a symbol we use one or two letters; the first letter of the symbol is always capitalized, the second is not. In some cases the symbol is similar to the name of the element. For example, the symbol for aluminum is Al. In many other cases it is not. The reason for the difference is that many elements have names taken from the ancient Latin and Greek languages. The Latin name for lead is plumbum. We get our word plumber from this word. The early scientists who were trained in Latin and Greek and used these terms assigned the symbol Pb to lead. Study the words listed below and learn some common elements and their symbols.

Element	Symbol	Element	Symbol
Aluminum	Al	Mercury	Hg
Antimony	Ab	Nickel	Ni
Arsenic	As	Nitrogen	N
Bromine	Br	Oxygen	O
Calcium	Ca	Phosphorous	P
Chlorine	Cl	Platinum	Pt
Copper	Cu	Potassium	K
Cobalt	Co	Radium	Ra
Gold	Au	Silicon	Si
Helium	He	Silver	Ag
Hydrogen	H	Sodium	Na
Iron	Fe	Sulfur	S
Iodine	I	Tin	Sn
Lead	Pb	Uranium	U
Magnesium	Mg	Zinc	Zn
Manganese	Mn		

ANCIENT NAMES FOR THE ELEMENTS

Plumbum

Natrium

Aurum

Stibium

Argentum

Hydrargyrum (Greek)

Kalium

Ferrum

This exercise will help you to remember the symbols of some elements which are not similar to their modern names. The elements listed above were named in ancient times by the early Romans and Greeks. Although we do not use these names, we have kept the symbols. How many of these ancient names can you match to their modern names and symbols given below?

MODERN NAME	SYMBOL	ANCIENT NAME
1. Antimony	Sb	_____
2. Gold	Au	_____
3. Iron	Fe	_____
4. Silver	Ag	_____
5. Sodium	Na	_____
6. Potassium	K	_____
7. Lead	Pb	_____
8. Mercury	Hg	_____

COMMON CHEMICALS IN OUR HOMES

COMMON CHEMICALS IN OUR HOMES

On the previous page are pictured some elements and compounds which are often found in homes. Listed below on the left are the common names and formulas. The scientific names for these substances are on the right. How many common names can you match to the scientific names? Use number answers.

1. Ammonia, NH_4OH ____ Silicon dioxide

2. Baking soda, $NaHCO_3$ ____ Hydrogen peroxide

3. Borax, $Na_2B_4O_7$ ____ Ammonium hydroxide

4. Chalk, $CaCo_3$ ____ Potassium bitartrate

5. Charcoal, C   ____ Calcium carbonate

6. Cream of tartar, $KHC_4H_4O_6$ ____ Sucrose

7. Diamond, C   ____ Magnesium hydroxide

8. Dry ice, CO_2 ____ Sodium bicarbonate

9. Epsom salts, $MgSO_4$ ____ Acetic acid

10. Flowers of sulfur, S   ____ Ethyl alcohol

11. Grain alcohol, C_2H_5OH ____ Sodium tetraborate

12. Graphite, C ("lead" in pencils)   ____ Potassium hydroxide or Sodium

                                              hydroxide

13. Lye, KOH or NaOH   ____ Sulfur

14. Milk of magnesia, $Mg(OH)_2$ ____ Carbon dioxide

15. Mothballs, $C_{10}H_8$ ____ Napthalene

16. Peroxide, H_2O_2 ____ Carbon

17. Table salt, NaCl   ____ Carbon

18. Sand, SiO_2 ____ Carbon

19. Table sugar, $C_{12}H_{22}O_{11}$ ____ Magnesium sulfate

20. Vinegar, CH_3COOH ____ Sodium chloride

THE ELEMENTS IN YOUR BODY

Your body's worth in terms of elements is only a few dollars even at inflated prices. Use the statistics below to make a bar graph on the next page showing the more common elements in an average human body.

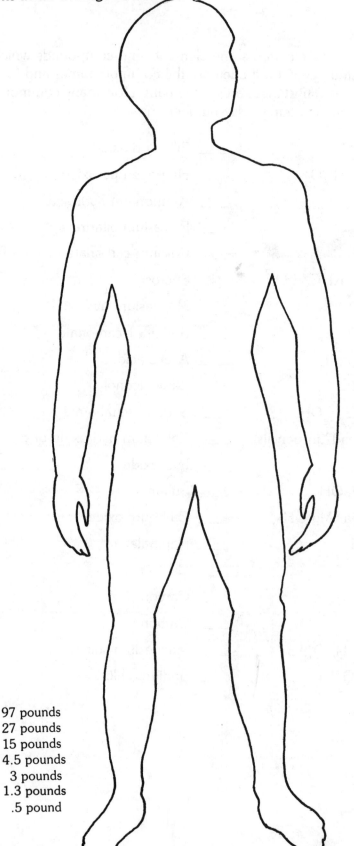

Oxygen	-	97 pounds
Carbon	-	27 pounds
Hydrogen	-	15 pounds
Nitrogen	-	4.5 pounds
Calcium	-	3 pounds
Phosphorus	-	1.3 pounds
Potassium	-	.5 pound

Sulfur	-	.5 pound
Sodium	-	.25 pound
Chlorine	-	.25 pound
Magnesium	-	.06 pound
Iodine	-	trace
Iron	-	trace
Others	-	traces

THE ELEMENTS IN YOUR BODY

Use the statistics on the previous page to fill in the bar graph below. You will be able to see at a glance the common elements in an average human body.

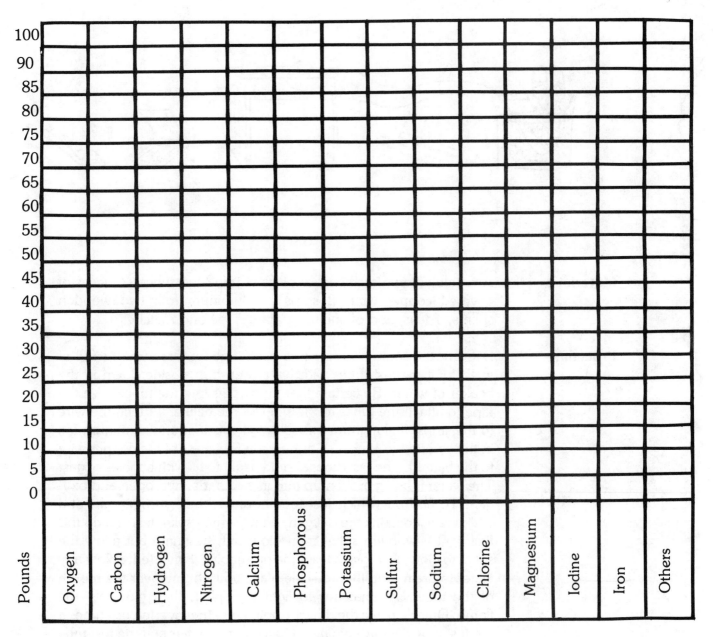

Elements

BREAKING A COMPOUND INTO ELEMENTS

In this activity you will take one of the most common compounds on earth, water (H_2O) and break it down into the two elements of which it is composed. The gases that compose water are oxygen, which supports combustion, and hydrogen, an explosive gas.

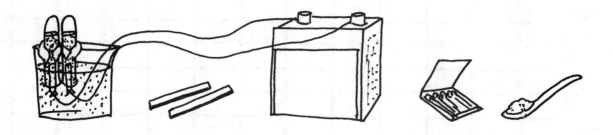

Materials: A 6 volt battery, large beaker or glass jar, 2 test tubes, 2 pieces of covered copper wire, 2 strips of aluminum foil, two wooden splints, 1 teaspoon of sodium sulfate, tape and matches.

Procedure: Dissolve the sodium sulfate in a beaker about three-fourths full of water. Fill the test tubes with water and turn upside down in the beaker of water. Be certain that no air gets into the tubes. Use the tape to attach the tubes to the sides of the beaker. Attach the wire to the strips of aluminum foil. Carefully position the aluminum foil in the inverted test tubes. Connect the free ends of the copper wire to the battery. The test tubes should begin to fill with bubbles of gas. The water is being broken up into its two parts, hydrogen and oxygen. To find out which test tube contains the hydrogen gas and which tube contains the oxygen, do a burning splint test. To do this first light a wooden splint then blow out the flame but allow the splint to glow. Remove a test tube by keeping it inverted. Allow any water to drain, and then quickly place your thumb over the mouth of the tube. Use matches to light the splint, then blow out the flame. Quickly place the glowing splint into the inverted test tube. If the test tube contains oxygen it will burst into flame; if the test tube contains hydrogen you will hear a loud "pop."

COMBINING TWO ELEMENTS
TO FORM A COMPOUND

The rusting of iron is a good example of a chemical change. When the element iron (Fe) rusts, it combines with the element oxygen (O) in the air to form a new compound iron oxide (Fe_2O_3). You will also observe in this experiment the amount of oxygen in the air used to rust the iron. For the element iron, we will use clean steel wool, which is mostly iron in a very fine form.

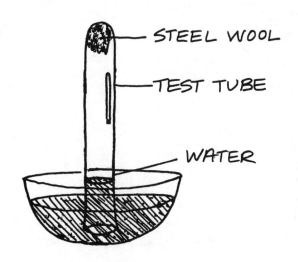

Materials: Tall glass or very large test tube, beaker or bowl, clean steel wool (not a soap pad) water.

Procedure: Pull a piece of steel wool apart to make it fluffy. Wet the steel wool and pack it into the bottom of a tall glass or test tube. Turn the test tube or glass upside down in a bowl or beaker which is half full of water. Set aside for two or three days.

Questions: 1. What happened to the steel wool?
                      2. What caused this to happen?
                      3. What happened to the water in the glass or test tube?
                      4. What two elements combined to form a new compound?
                      5. What is the name of the new compound?

AIR,
A MIXTURE OF GASES

Air is a mixture of several elements and compounds in a gaseous form. The various gases in the air vary from time to time and place to place as the gaseous state of water or humidity in the air does. In many places pollutants, dust and pollen are also mixed in the air. To show at a glance the amounts of the gases that are in the air, put the following information in the circle graph below.

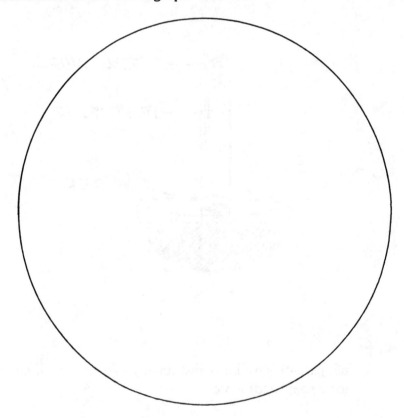

GASES IN THE AIR IN PERCENT BY VOLUME

Nitrogen	(N)	78%
Oxygen	(O)	20%
Argon	(Ar)	1%
Carbon dioxide	(CO_2)	.03%
Traces of Neon	(Ne) Helium (He), Krypton (Kr), Xenon (Xe), Radon (Rn),	
	and water vapor (H_2O).	

THE PERIODIC TABLE

The Periodic Table is a system which helps to classify the elements. In 1735 there were only 13 known elements; in 1850 there were 47; today there are over 100 including several man-made elements. The Periodic Table that we use today was devised by a Russian scientist named Dmitri Mendeleev in 1869.

A Periodic Table can tell us many things; in it the elements are arranged in order of their atomic numbers, which is the number of protons in the nucleus of a particular element. The atomic weight or mass of an element, that is, its total number of protons and neutrons, is also given, as well as its name and symbol.

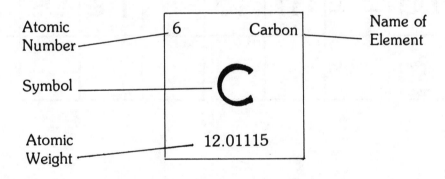

The horizontal rows on a Periodic Table are called periods, and the vertical rows are called groups. All of the elements in a group have similar characteristics; for example, the elements in the last group - helium, neon, argon, krypton, xenon, and radon are all inactive gases.

You will also notice the elements on the far left, with the exception of hydrogen, are metals.

THE PERIODIC TABLE

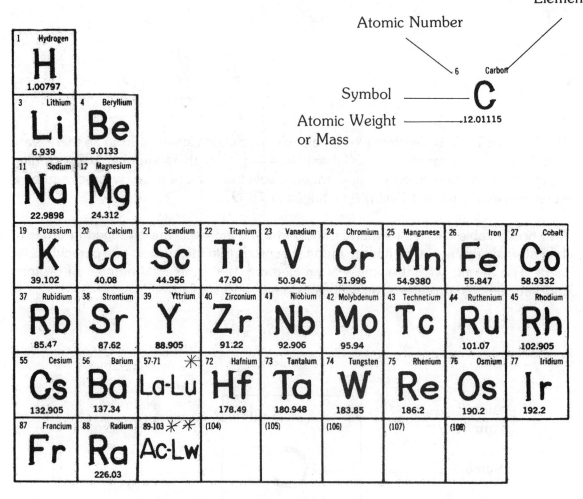

						2 Helium **He** 4.0026
5 Boron **B** 10.811	6 Carbon **C** 12.01115	7 Nitrogen **N** 14.0067	8 Oxygen **O** 15.9994	9 Fluorine **F** 18.9984	10 Neon **Ne** 20.183
13 Aluminum **Al** 26.9815	14 Silicon **Si** 28.086	15 Phosphorus **P** 30.9738	16 Sulfur **S** 32.064	17 Chlorine **Cl** 35.453	18 Argon **Ar** 39.948

28 Nickel **Ni** 58.71	29 Copper **Cu** 63.54	30 Zinc **Zn** 65.37	31 Gallium **Ga** 69.72	32 Germanium **Ge** 72.59	33 Arsenic **As** 74.9216	34 Selenium **Se** 78.96	35 Bromine **Br** 79.909	36 Krypton **Kr** 83.80
46 Palladium **Pd** 106.4	47 Silver **Ag** 107.870	48 Cadmium **Cd** 112.40	49 Indium **In** 114.82	50 Tin **Sn** 118.69	51 Antimony **Sb** 121.75	52 Tellurium **Te** 127.60	53 Iodine **I** 126.9044	54 Xenon **Xe** 131.30
78 Platinum **Pt** 195.09	79 Gold **Au** 196.967	80 Mercury **Hg** 200.59	81 Thallium **Tl** 204.37	82 Lead **Pb** 207.19	83 Bismuth **Bi** 208.980	84 Polonium **Po**	85 Astatine **At**	86 Radon **Rn**

64 Gadolinium **Gd** 157.25	65 Terbium **Tb** 158.924	66 Dysprosium **Dy** 162.50	67 Holmium **Ho** 164.930	68 Erbium **Er** 167.26	69 Thulium **Tm** 168.934	70 Ytterbium **Yb** 173.04	71 Lutetium **Lu** 174.97
96 Curium **Cm**	97 Berkelium **Bk**	98 Californium **Cf**	99 Einsteinium **E**	100 Fermium **Fm**	101 Mendelevium **Mv**	102 **102**	(103) **Lw**

HOW ELEMENTS ARE NAMED

Study the Periodic Chart of the elements on pages 30 and 31. Do any of the names of the elements sound familiar? They should. Some elements have ancient names of Latin and Greek origins; but many others were named for famous men, countries, planets, etc. With a copy of the Periodic Chart before you, see how many of the following questions you can answer:

1. There are five elements named for famous scientists. Can you find three?
   _____ , _____ and _____ .

2. There are four elements named for planets. Can you find all four of them?
   _____ , _____ , _____ , and _____ .

3. There is one element named for a city in the United States and another for the state of that city. Can you find the element named for the city and the element named for the state? _____ and _____ .

4. There are two elements named for large regions which include several countries. Do you know what these elements are called? _____ and _____ .

5. Element numbers 68, 70, 39, and 65 were all named for the same city, Ytterby, Sweden. What are the names of these elements?
   _____ , _____ , _____ , and _____ .

6. The ancient name for France was Gaul, and the ancient name for Russia was Ruthenia. Can you find the elements named for these ancient lands?
   _____ and _____ .

7. Find the elements named in honor of France, America, Poland and Germany.
   _____ , _____ , _____ and _____ .

ELEMENT BINGO!

Learn the symbols of the elements by playing Element Bingo! Fill in the card below with the symbols of your favorite elements. When your teacher calls out the NAME of the element, cross out the symbol on your card. When you have a row crossed out, call Element Bingo!

Variation: Try playing Blackout Bingo by crossing out the entire card.

Note to Teacher: You may wish to have students play Element Bingo with a copy of the periodic chart before them as a guide. After the students have learned the symbols, they can play Element Bingo without the aid of a periodic table.

USING OXYGEN FOR BURNING

The element oxygen makes up about 20 percent of the atmosphere. Oxygen itself does not burn, but it is necessary for the burning of other materials. We say that "oxygen supports combustion." To show how this is done, do the following experiment:

Materials: Candle, bowl, glass or jar, matches, water.

Procedure: Light the candle and melt a little wax along the lip of the candle to use for attaching it to the bowl. Add water to the bowl and cover the burning candle with the glass or jar. Observe for a few minutes; answer the questions below.

Questions: 1. What happened to the candle? Why?
2. Why did the water rise in the glass?
3. What distance did the water rise?

ACIDS

Acids are compounds which contain the element hydrogen (H) and change blue litmus paper to red. Litmus paper is called an indicator by scientists because it indicates or tells a scientist at a glance whether a substance is an acid or a base. Many foods we eat are mildly acidic. You can tell this because acids in food have a sour taste. Oranges, lemons, limes, and grapefruits contain citric acid. Vinegar contains acetic acid. Strong acids such as sulfuric and nitric acids are very dangerous to handle. Below are the names of some common acids and their formulas.

BLUE LITMUS TURNS RED

VINEGAR

Sulfuric acid	- H_2SO_4
Hydrochloric acid	- HCl
Nitric acid	- HNO_3
Acetic acid	- $HC_2H_3O_2$

1. What 3 elements are found in sulfuric acid?

_____   _____   _____

2. What 2 elements are found in hydrochloric acid?

_____   _____

3. What 3 elements are found in nitric acid?

_____   _____   _____

4. What 3 elements are found in acetic acid?

_____   _____   _____

5. Which element is found in all acids? _____

USE CABBAGE TO MAKE AN ACID

Cabbage changes into sauerkraut by the action of bacteria and the production of lactic acid. Salt is used to draw the natural sugar and water out of cabbage leaves enabling the lactic acid bacteria to convert the sugar into lactic acid. The lactic acid gives the sauerkraut its unusual taste.

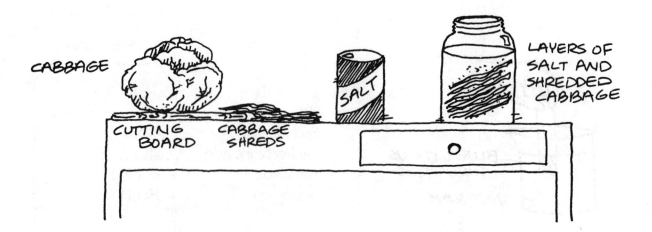

Materials: Cabbage, salt, knife, cutting board, jar, and water.

Procedure: Shred the cabbage until you have about two cups of finely sliced leaves. Pack ½ cup of cabbage into a jar or similar container. Sprinkle cabbage leaves with salt. Use about one-eighth to one-fourth teaspoon of salt for each ½ cup of cabbage. Add another layer of cabbage leaves and sprinkle again with salt. Repeat the layering process until all the cabbage is in the jar. Press the cabbage into the jar until firmly packed. Add water to barely cover the cabbage.* Put cover over the jar, but do not tightly cap. Leave undisturbed at room temperature for about two weeks; you will then have sauerkraut.

You may wish to test the sauerkraut for acidity with litmus paper.

Questions:
1. What ingredients are needed to make sauerkraut?
2. What is the function of salt in the making of sauerkraut?
3. Can sauerkraut be easily made at home?
4. What other foods are made by the action of helpful bacteria?
5. What is the source of the lactic acid in bacteria?

*Continue to add water to just cover the cabbage as it evaporates.

BASES

Bases are compounds which contain the elements oxygen and hydrogen grouped together; we call this grouping a hydroxide (OH). Bases turn red litmus blue and have a slippery feeling when touched. Strong bases such as lye are very dangerous to handle. Below are the names and formulas of some common bases:

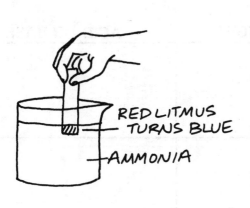

RED LITMUS
TURNS BLUE

AMMONIA

BASE	FORMULA
Ammonia	NH_4OH
Sodium hydroxide	NaOH (lye)
Magnesium hydroxide	$Mg(OH)_2$ (milk of magnesia)
Calcium hydroxide	$Ca(OH)_2$ (limewater)

Questions:
1. What two elements in addition to the hydroxide group are found in ammonia?
2. What element in addition to the hydroxide group is found in lye?
3. What element is found in milk of magnesia in addition to the hydroxide group?
4. What two elements are found in all bases?
5. What is this grouping called?

ACID OR BASE?

Gather some common household items and test them to find out whether they are acids or bases.

Materials: Red and blue litmus paper, lemon juice, pickle juice, milk of magnesia, window cleaner, salad dressing, liquid soap, etc.

Procedure: Use a small amount of a variety of household substances to determine whether they are acids or bases. Keep a record of your findings. Remember that acids turn blue litmus red and bases turn red litmus blue.

SUBSTANCE	LITMUS CHANGE	ACID OR BASE?
PICKLES		
MILK OF MAGNESIA		
LIQUID SOAP		
GLASS CLEANER		
LEMON		
ITALIAN SALAD DRESSING		

MAKING AN INDICATOR

Litmus paper is called an indicator by chemists because it indicates whether or not a substance is an acid or base. It is made by extracting a vegetable dye from plants and soaking strips of paper in the dye. The paper is then dried and packaged. You can make an effective indicator by using the dye found in red cabbage leaves. Try the following experiment to test your homemade indicator.

Materials: Red cabbage leaves, ammonia, vinegar, rubbing alcohol, test tubes, white construction paper, beaker or jar.

Procedure: Thinly slice about a cup of red cabbage leaves and put them into a beaker or jar. Add enough rubbing alcohol to cover the leaves and allow them to soak several hours. Drain off the liquid. Discard the cabbage leaves. Pour a little of the liquid into a test tube and add a common household acid such as lemon juice or vinegar. Notice the color change. Pour some of the liquid into another test tube and add a common household base such as ammonia. Notice the color change. Experiment by adding some of the vinegar solution to the ammonia solution and vice versa.

Variation: You can use your alcohol-cabbage solution to make indicator strips of your own by soaking strips of white construction paper in the alcohol-cabbage solution and then allowing the strips to dry thoroughly. Use the strips to test vinegar and ammonia.

MAKING AN INDICATOR

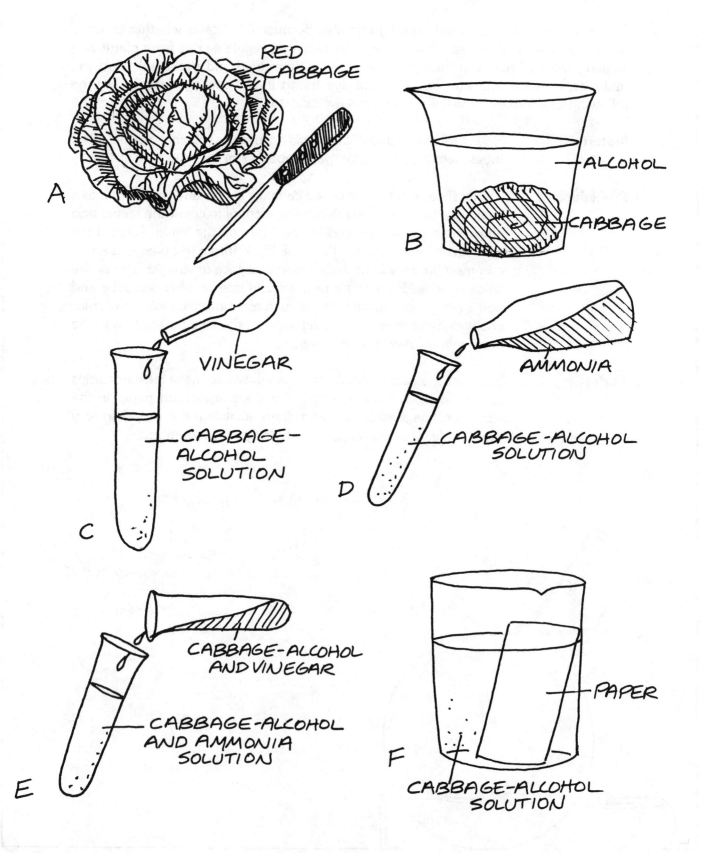

A RED CABBAGE

B ALCOHOL
   CABBAGE

C VINEGAR
   CABBAGE-ALCOHOL SOLUTION

D AMMONIA
   CABBAGE-ALCOHOL SOLUTION

E CABBAGE-ALCOHOL AND VINEGAR
   CABBAGE-ALCOHOL AND AMMONIA SOLUTION

F PAPER
   CABBAGE-ALCOHOL SOLUTION

WHAT IS A PRECIPITATE?

To a chemist, precipitation is the result of a chemical change in which a substance falls in a solution. Many valuable chemical products are formed as precipitates. To show how precipitates are formed, do the following experiment:

Materials: Epsom salts (can be purchased at a drug store), ammonia, beaker, water.

Procedure: Put 2 or 3 tablespoons of epsom salts into a beaker. Add ½ cup of water. Stir until the epsom salts are dissolved. Add about a cup of household ammonia. (Add more ammonia if necessary.) A white precipitate will form. The chemical equation for the experiment you have just done is:

$$MgSO_4 + 2NH_4OH \rightarrow Mg(OH)_2 \downarrow + (NH_4)_2SO_4$$

| Epsom salts | + | ammonia | $\rightarrow$ | magnesium↓ hydroxide | + | ammonia sulfate |

The magnesium hydroxide is insoluble (will not dissolve) from the ammonia sulfate and can be separated be filtering. The common name for magnesium hydroxide is milk of magnesia. The arrow pointing down in an equation tells a chemist that a precipitate has been formed.

EMULSIFIERS

An emulsifier is a substance that breaks down fats, grease and oils. When you use soap you are using an emulsifier. The soap acts on the natural oils of your skin to remove the dirt which has collected. The making of soap is a simple process. Pioneers made their own soap as some people still do. They saved the fats left over from cooking, and from their wood fires they obtained lye (sodium hydroxide) by pouring water through the ashes. This water was saved and boiled with the fat to make soap. Modern soap is still made from oils and strong bases such as lye, but now most of the impurities are removed and color and perfume are often added. The soap is then cut into cakes, packaged and sold.

Here are some emulsifiers used in homes. Can you list others?

AN EMULSIFIER FOR EATING

Mayonnaise is made by the action of an emulsifier. It is usually bought in a grocery store as are other emulsifiers such as soap. You can make your own mayonnaise which will illustrate the action of an emulsifier in foods and have a product which has no artificial coloring or preservatives by following the recipe below.

Materials:

1 egg
½ teaspoon of salt
2 tablespoons of lemon juice
½ teaspoon of mustard
1 cup of soybean oil
Add the oil slowly, ¼ cup at a time.

Procedure:

Blend all ingredients at low speed. Be sure to add the oil gradually. This recipe must be refrigerated.

Question:

Oil and lemon juice do not usually mix. Do you know what item in the recipe was the emulsifier?

SOLUTIONS

The knowledge and uses of solutions are very important in the study of chemistry. A solution is made when one substance dissolves in another. The substance which does the dissolving is called the *solvent*; the substance which is dissolved is the *solute*. When hot tea or coffee is sweetened with sugar, a solution is made. In this case the hot tea or coffee is the solvent; the sugar is the solute. Salt will dissolve in hot soup to become a solution; pepper will not. Most solutions are made when solids are dissolved in liquids, but this is not the only kind of solution. Liquids will dissolve in other liquids as alcohol will dissolve in water. Gases can sometimes be made to dissolve in liquids as in the example of carbon dioxide in soft drinks. If a material will not dissolve in another substance, we say that it is *insoluble*.

COFFEE   TEA   SOUP

Questions: 1. Which of the above are solvents?
2. Which are solutes?
3. Which ones will be solutions?
4. Which substance is insoluble?

SOLUTIONS

Circle the word "yes" if the picture in the box represents a solution; "no" if it does not.

YES   NO   YES   NO   YES   NO

OIL
VINEGAR

WATER
SAND

IODINE

YES   NO   YES   NO   YES   NO

CARBON
DIOXIDE
GAS

CLEANING
FLUID

YES   NO   YES   NO   YES   NO

MELTED
WAX

JELLY

SUGAR

TESTING FOR SOLUBILITY

WATER   POLISH REMOVER   PAINT THINNER   ALCOHOL

Materials: Wax crayon, water, nail polish remover, paint thinner, alcohol, four beakers or jars.

Procedure: Label the beakers, A, B, C, and D. Add a small piece of crayon to each beaker. Into beaker A pour enough water to cover the crayon. Add nail polish remover to beaker B, paint thinner to beaker C, and alcohol to beaker D. Allow to stand overnight or longer. Answer the questions below and fill in the chart at the bottom of the page.

Questions:
1. Are cleaning fluids usually good solvents? Why?
2. List some solvents which you use in everyday life.
3. Can you think of instances when solvents can do more harm than good?

BEAKER	SOLUTION	NOT A SOLUTION	SOLVENT	SOLUTE
A				
B				
C				
D				

ROCK CANDY CRYSTALS

Crystals are formed when a fluid becomes a solid. They have definite geometric shapes, and the crystals of a particular substance are always the same. The study of crystals is a very important part of chemistry. One way it has aided scientists is in their discoveries of the sizes and shapes of many atoms and molecules. Table salt and sugar are two familiar crystals. You can make some crystals of your own if you follow the directions below.

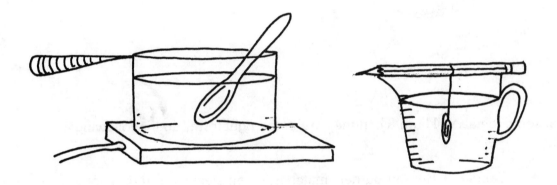

Materials: ½ cup of water, 1 cup of sugar, pan, measuring cup, heat source, such as a hot plate, pencil, string, small weight, such as a paper clip, spoon.

Procedure: Slowly add ½ cup of the sugar to the water in the pan, a teaspoon at a time. Stir until the sugar dissolves. Heat the sugar water in the pan and continue to add sugar, teaspoon by teaspoon, as the water is heating until all the sugar is dissolved. Continue to heat until the mixture begins to boil. Boil for a couple of minutes. Mixture should be clear and thick. Pour into a pyrex container. Drop a weighted string into the solution, and place in a spot where it will be undisturbed. When the crystals are large enough, remove and taste. These are rock candy crystals. The evaporation of the water helps the crystals to grow. It may take several weeks for large crystals to form. If a crust forms, carefully remove it so that the water continues to evaporate.

CAN METALS BURN?

To show that some metals will burn when they are in the right form, do the following experiment:

Materials: Candle or Bunsen burner, matches, clean steel wool (not a soap pad).

Procedure: Pull the steel wool apart so that it is not bunched. With pliers or tongs, hold the steel wool over the flame of a lighted candle. The steel wool will burn.
Another example of a metal that will burn is magnesium. Obtain some magnesium ribbon from a chemical supply house. With pliers or tongs, hold a 3" to 4" piece of magnesium ribbon over a flame. The flame will be very, very bright. AVOID LOOKING AT IT DIRECTLY. It may hurt your eyes.

Questions: 1. In what form must the iron (steel wool) be before it will burn?
2. In what form was the magnesium?
3. Do you think either metal would burn if it were in thick heavy slices or chunks? Why?

COPPER COATING A NAIL

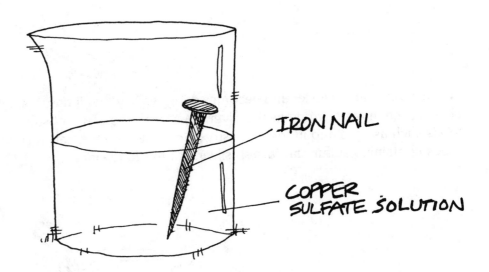

IRON NAIL

COPPER SULFATE SOLUTION

In this experiment you will see how a metal (iron) can replace another metal (copper) when it is placed in a solution containing a salt (copper sulfate) of that metal.

Materials: A clean iron nail, copper sulfate crystals, water, a beaker, fine sandpaper.

Procedure: Use the sandpaper to clean the nail thoroughly. Dissolve a teaspoon of copper sulfate in about ½ cup of water. Distilled water is best, if available. Put one or two nails in the copper sulfate solution. Allow them to stand several hours or overnight.

Questions: 1. Describe the appearance of the nail after standing in the copper sulfate solution.
2. What changes appeared in the copper sulfate solution?
3. Complete this sentence: Some of the copper has left the solution and is now _____ .
4. Complete this sentence: Some of the iron has left the nail and is now _____ .
5. Is this experiment an example of a physical or chemical change?

WHAT MAKES SILVER TARNISH?

When silver loses its luster and becomes dark, we say that it has tarnished. This is the result of a chemical change occurring as the silver reacts with the element sulfur. Sulfur is found in certain foods such as eggs and in the air in small amounts as a gas called sulfur dioxide. To show how foods containing sulfur can tarnish silver, do the following:

Materials: An article made of silver or silver plate (such as a spoon), egg, beaker or cup.

Procedure: Separate the yolk from the white of the egg. Retain the yolk in the beaker. Place the silver article or spoon in the egg yolk and stir. Allow the spoon to remain in the egg yolk about ten minutes. Remove, rinse and examine.

Questions:
1. Describe the appearance of the spoon.
2. Silver plus sulfur equals silver sulfide. Explain.
3. Why do you think the silver in the egg yolk tarnished so quickly?
4. Is the tarnishing of silver the result of a physical or chemical change? Why?

ISOTOPES

Isotopes are different forms of the same element. All elements have at least two isotopes; some elements have more. Isotopes occur when the atoms of an element have the same number of protons and electrons but different numbers of neutrons. This means that the isotopes of an element will all have the same atomic number but different atomic mass or weight.

EXAMPLES OF TWO ISOTOPES OF HYDROGEN

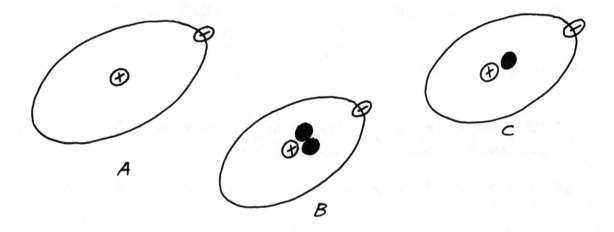

Some elements such as radium and uranium have isotopes which give off particles; we say these elements are radioactive. Radioactive elements give off large amounts of radiation in very short spaces of time. These particles can be heard as clicks on an instrument called a Geiger counter. Although radioactive elements are very dangerous, many uses have been found for them in medicine and industry.

ISOTOPES

1. What is isotope?

2. What do we call an isotope that gives off particles?

3. Name two elements whose isotopes give off particles.

4. Do isotopes of the same element have the same atomic weight?

5. Do isotopes of the same element have the same atomic number?

6. What instrument measures radioactivity?

7. What are the atomic weights of two isotopes of the element hydrogen?

8. All the isotopes of hydrogen have the same number of which atomic parts?

9. All of the isotopes of hydrogen have a different number of which atomic part?

10. Can you list some ways in which radioactive elements can be dangerous?

11. Where are radioactive elements used for the good of mankind?

12. Make a list of ways in which radioactive elements are used.

WHAT IS HALF-LIFE?

You have heard the expression that cats have nine lives, but do you know what it means when a chemist refers to the half-life of an element or isotope? Half-life is the amount of time it takes for one gram of an element to lose *half* its radioactivity.

As radioactive elements lose particles, they change from one element to another; because they are changing, we say that they are unstable. Radioactive or unstable elements keep changing until they become stable. Uranium is an example of an unstable element which changes into the other unstable elements - ionium, radium, radon, and polonium - before it becomes lead, a stable element. Do the following experiment to help you understand the half-life of radioactive elements.

Materials: Paper punch and construction paper, any color.

Procedure: Punch out exactly 128 holes. The 128 punches represent atomic particles in one gram of a radioactive element that we will call Cobbium. Cobbium has a half-life of 50 years. Separate half of 128 or 64 punches and put these aside, they represent the radioactive particles being given off by Cobbium in the first 50 years. Now separate half of the remaining 64 particles; put these aside with the first group of punches you took out. Continue to keep separating out half of the remaining particles and keep track of the time it takes for the element to become stable by adding 50 years each time you remove half of the punches.

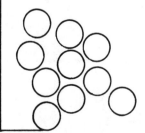

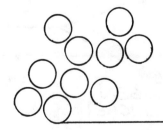

FISSION AND FUSION

Before scientists could break up an atom, they first had to find a suitable "bullet" which could enter and split the nucleus of the atom. They thought of using a proton, but protons have positive charges, and they would not be allowed to enter the nucleus as they would be repelled by the protons already present in the nucleus. Scientists also considered using an electron, but electrons are too tiny to do the job. Next, they considered a neutron. Neutrons are large enough and they do not have a charge; so that is exactly what they used. When the atom was split by using the neutron "bullet," a huge amount of energy was released. One element chosen for splitting was an isotope of uranium called U-235. When a uranium nucleus with an atomic weight of 235 was split, the results were one isotope of barium nucleus, one isotope of krypton nucleus, two free neutrons, and an enormous amount of energy. This is atomic fission.

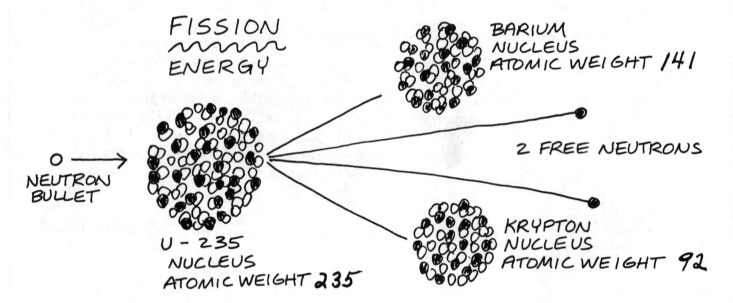

Atomic scientists later learned that more energy is released when the two nuclei of a light element, such as an isotope of hydrogen, combine or fuse to make the heavier element, helium. This is known as atomic fusion.

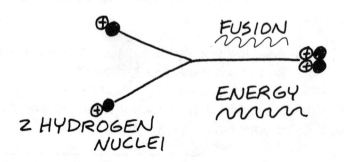

A CHAIN REACTION

When a uranium (U-235) atom is split there is released an enormous amount of energy along with three by-products: an atom each of the elements barium and krypton, plus two free neutrons. These two free neutrons can act as bullets and go on to split other atoms of U-235. This fission or atom-splitting will continue at a faster and faster pace setting up a chain reaction. The control of nuclear fission in chain reactions is accomplished by the use of neutron-absorbing materials in control rods. To illustrate how a chain reaction works, do the following experiment:

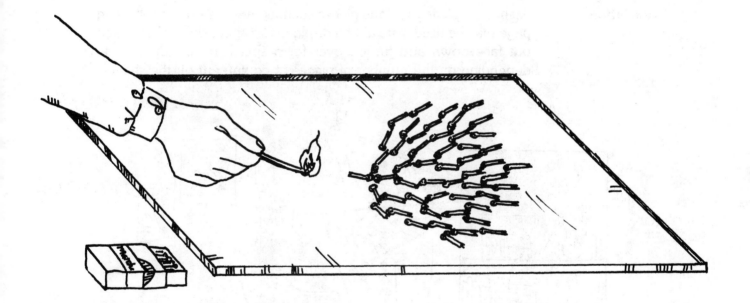

Materials: Box of wooden matchsticks, cookie sheet.

Procedure: Break the tips off several wooden matchsticks and arrange them on cookie sheet as illustrated. Light the first match and watch the results.

Questions: 1. What does the first match represent in a chain reaction?
2. What do the other matches represent?
3. What stopped or controlled this chain reaction?
4. What is used to stop or control a real nuclear chain reaction?
5. What is your definition of a chain reaction?

SCIENCE MEMORY

While studying chemistry, a simple memory quiz can be fun. This exercise can also help students become acquainted with the uses of various pieces of science equipment.

Materials: About 20 pieces of familiar equipment normally found in a science class. Good articles for this exercise are: a test tube, Bunsen burner, petri dish, watch glass, mortar and pestle, scalpel, scissors, probe, test tube holder, graduated cylinder, Erlenmeyer flask, Florence flask, eyedropper, slide, cover slip, microscope, etc.

Procedure: Be sure students are familiar with the names of the equipment. Display the equipment where it is visible to all members of the class. Allow the students to study the equipment for two or three minutes. Cover. Ask students to list as many items as they can remember.

Variation: A sheet depicting various pieces such as the one on the following page may be used instead of a display. The sheet should be passed out face down and turned over for a specified amount of time depending on the number of pieces of equipment on the sheet.

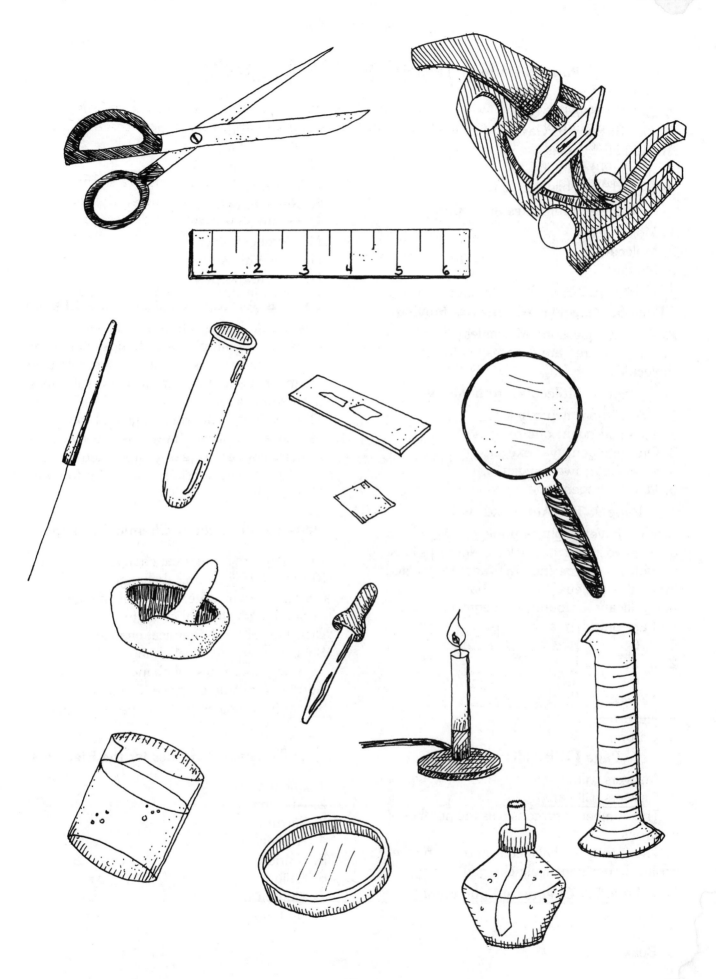

Answer Key

Page 2: Matter

1. Solid 2. Gas 3. Solid
4. Solid 5. Solid 6. Gas
7. Gas 8. Solid 9. Gas
10. Liquid 11. Gas
12. Solid 13. Liquid
14. Solid 15. Solid 16. Liquid

Page 4: Molecules and Matter

1. Molecules
2. Molecule
3. Moving
4. Differ

Page 5: Molecules Are Always Moving

Answer to question: Molecules are always moving; there are spaces between the molecules.

Page 7: Molecules from Atoms

1. One carbon; two oxygen
2. Two hydrogen; one oxygen
3. One nitrogen; two oxygen
4. One sulfur; two oxygen
5. One hydrogen; one chlorine

Page 9: The Atom and Its Parts

Protons have weight, a positive charge, and are located inside the nucleus. Neutrons have weight, no charge (neutral), and are located inside the nucleus. Electrons have no weight (insignificant amount), a negative charge, and are outside the nucleus.

1. 2, 6
2. 6, 2
3. 2, 6
4. 12, 4
5. Helium
6. Carbon

Page 11: Building Atoms

1. Answers will vary.
2. Answers will vary.
3. The number of protons plus the number of neutrons.
4. The atom is balanced and is neither positively nor negatively charged.

Page 12: Chemistry Equipment

A. Tongs
B. Pipette
C. Beaker
D. Test tube
E. Test tube holder
F. Clamp
G. Ring stand
H. Bunsen burner
 I. Graduated cylinder
J. Test tube brush
K. Reagent bottle
L. Erlenmeyer flask
M. Florence flasks
N. Watch glass
O. Mortar and pestle

Page 18: A Physical and Chemical Change

The simple mixing of the iron filings and the sulfur is an example of a physical change as the two substances are easily separated by the magnet and no chemically new substance has been formed.

The heating of the iron filings and the sulfur caused a chemical change as the two substances cannot be easily separated by the magnet. A new substance has been formed, iron sulfide.

Page 19: Physical or Chemical Change?

Crushing a rock-physical change
Rusting of iron-chemical change
Seltzer tablet in water-chemical change
Slicing bread-physical change
Digestion of food-chemical change
Baking bread-chemical change
Tearing paper-physical change
Burning a candle-chemical change
Steam from boiling water-physical change

Page 21: Ancient Names for the Elements

1. Stibium
2. Aurum
3. Ferrum
4. Argentum
5. Natrium
6. Kalium
7. Plumbum
8. Hydrargyrum

Page 23: Common Chemicals in Our Homes

18 Silicon dioxide
16 Hydrogen peroxide
 1 Ammonium hydroxide
 6 Potassium bitartrate
 4 Calcium carbonate
19 Sucrose
14 Magnesium hydroxide
 2 Sodium bicarbonate
20 Acetic acid
11 Ethyl alcohol
 3 Sodium tetraborate
13 Potassium hydroxide or Sodium
     hydroxide
10 Sulfur
 8 Carbon dioxide
15 Napthalene
 5, 7, 12 Carbon
 5, 7, 12 Carbon
 5, 7, 12 Carbon
 9 Magnesium sulfate
17 Sodium chloride

Page 27: Combining Two Elements to Form a Compound

1. It rusted.
2. The iron in the steel wool combined with the oxygen in the air to form iron oxide or rust.
3. It rose.
4. Iron and oxygen
5. Iron oxide

Page 32: How Elements Are Named

1. Mendelevium #101 named for Dmitri Mendeleev.
   Curium #96 named for Pierre and Marie Curie.
   Einsteinium #99 named for Albert Einstein.
   Fermium #100 named for Enrico Fermi.
   Lawrencium #103 named for Ernest Lawrence.

2. Mercury #80, Neptunium #93, Plutonium #94 and Uranium #92.
3. Berkelium #97 for Berkeley; and Californium #98 for California.
4. Europium #63 and Scandium #21.

5. Erbium #68, Ytterbium #70, Yttrium #39 and Terbium #65 are all named in honor of Ytterby, Sweden.
6. Gallium #31, Ruthenium #44.
7. Francium #87, Americium #95, Polonium #84 and Germanium #32.

Page 34: Using Oxygen for Burning

1. The candle went out due to lack of oxygen.
2. The water took the place of the oxygen.
3. Less than 20% of the way.

Page 35: Acids

1. Hydrogen, sulfur, and oxygen
2. Hydrogen, chlorine
3. Hydrogen, nitrogen, and oxygen
4. Hydrogen, carbon and oxygen
5. Hydrogen

Page 36: Use Cabbage to Make an Acid

1. Cabbage, salt, water.
2. To draw the juice out of the cabbage.
3. Yes.
4. Cheese, wine.
5. Lactic acid bacteria are in the air.

Page 37: Bases

1. Nitrogen, hydrogen
2. Sodium
3. Magnesium
4. Oxygen and hydrogen
5. The hydroxide group

Page 38: Acid or Base?

Pickles change blue litmus to red, acid.
Milk of magnesia changes red litmus to blue, base.
Liquid soap changes red litmus to blue, base.
Glass cleaner (ammonia) changes red litmus to blue, base.
Lemon changes blue litmus to red, acid.
Italian salad dressing (vinegar) changes blue litmus to red, acid.

Page 43: An Emulsifier for Eating

Question: The egg was the emulsifier. Specifically, the yolk of the egg.

Page 44: Solutions

1. Coffee, tea, soup
2. Sugar, salt
3. Coffee and sugar, tea and sugar, soup and salt
4. Pepper

Page 45: Solutions

Vinegar and oil, no
Sand and water, no
Iodine, yes
Pepper and soup, no
Cola, yes
Cleaning fluid, yes
Wax on jelly, no
Sugar in tea or coffee, yes
Salt in soup, yes

Page 46: Testing for Solubility

Beaker A is not a solution.
Beaker B is a solution, the polish remover is the solvent, the crayon is the solute.
Beaker C is a solution, the paint thinner is the solvent, the crayon is the solute.
Beaker D is a solution, the alcohol is the solvent, the crayon is the solute. Note: The paint thinner was the best solvent; the nail polish remover was second best; and the alcohol third.

Page 48: Can Metals Burn?

1. Very fine as in steel wool.
2. A very thin ribbon.
3. No. It would be too difficult to combine with the oxygen necessary for burning and too difficult to heat unless it is thin.

Page 49: Copper Coating a Nail

1. Rusty
2. No longer bright blue
3. Coating the nail
4. Part of the solution
5. Chemical. New substances have been formed.

Page 50: What Makes Silver Tarnish?

1. Dark and tarnished.
2. Silver atoms combine with sulfur atoms to form a new compound.
3. There was a great deal of sulfur in the egg yolk which could easily combine with the silver.
4. Chemical. A new substance has been formed, the compound silver sulfide.

Page 52: Isotopes

1. Isotopes are different forms of the same element.
2. Radioactive
3. Radium, uranium
4. No
5. Yes
6. A Geiger counter
7. Hydrogen 3 and hydrogen 2
8. Electrons and protons
9. Neutrons
10. Answers will vary. Exposure to high level radiation has been known to cause cancer.
11. Answers will vary. Medicine and industry use radioactive elements as tracers, to treat tumors, to power nuclear plants and submarines, etc.
12. Answers will vary.

Page 55: A Chain Reaction

1. The neutron bullet.
2. Atoms of uranium 235.
3. All the matches were used.
4. Control rods, amount of uranium used.
5. Answers will vary.